CAREERS MAKING A DIFFERENCE

HELPING CHILDREN

CAREERS MAKING A DIFFERENCE

HELPING ANIMALS

HELPING CHILDREN

HELPING SENIORS

HELPING THOSE IN POVERTY

HELPING THOSE WITH ADDICTIONS

HELPING THOSE WITH DISABILITIES

HELPING THOSE WITH MENTAL ILLNESSES

HELPING TO PROTECT THE ENVIRONMENT

HELPING VICTIMS

CAREERS MAKING A DIFFERENCE

HELPING CHILDREN

AMANDA TURNER

MASON CREST

PHILADELPHIA
MIAMI

MASON CREST

450 Parkway Drive, Suite D, Broomall, Pennsylvania 19008
(866) MCP-BOOK (toll-free) • www.masoncrest.com

Printed in the United States of America

First printing
9 8 7 6 5 4 3 2 1

ISBN (hardback) 978-1-4222-4255-1
ISBN (series) 978-1-4222-4253-7
ISBN (ebook) 978-1-4222-7541-2

Cataloging-in-Publication Data on file with the Library of Congress

NATIONAL HIGHLIGHTS

Developed and produced by National Highlights Inc.
Editor: Susan Uttendorfsky
Interior and cover design: Torque Advertising + Design
Production: Michelle Luke

TABLE OF CONTENTS

KEY ICONS TO LOOK FOR

Words to Understand: These words with their easy-to-understand definitions will increase the reader's understanding of the text while building vocabulary skills.

Sidebars: This boxed material within the main text allows readers to build knowledge, gain insights, explore possibilities, and broaden their perspectives by weaving together additional information to provide realistic and holistic perspectives.

Educational Videos: Readers can view videos by scanning our QR codes, providing them with additional educational content to supplement the text. Examples include news coverage, moments in history, speeches, iconic sports moments, and much more!

Text-Dependent Questions: These questions send the reader back to the text for more careful attention to the evidence presented there.

Research Projects: Readers are pointed toward areas of further inquiry connected to each chapter. Suggestions are provided for projects that encourage deeper research and analysis.

Series Glossary of Key Terms: This back-of-the-book glossary contains terminology used throughout this series. Words found here increase the reader's ability to read and comprehend higher-level books and articles in this field.

AWARENESS OF THE CAUSE

In an advanced society such as the United States, we expect all children to have a reasonable standard of living, to be properly educated, and receive appropriate health care. However, there are times when children suffer from neglect, poverty, or abuse. Professionals who make a career in helping children make it their responsibility to enhance the lives of all children regardless of their wealth, religion, or race.

"There can be no keener revelation of a society's soul than the way in which it treats its children."
– Nelson Mandela

"The best way to make children good is to make them happy."
– Oscar Wilde

"Children are our most valuable resource."
– Herbert Hoover

"It is easier to build strong children than to repair broken men."
– Frederick Douglass

CHAPTER

Is a Career Helping Children for You?

Most people have a worthy cause that they believe in. You can even work in this field yourself by following a career and making a difference to those in need.

- Start out as a volunteer.
- Seek out a personal connection in the field.
- Develop an inspirational mission statement for yourself.
- Find out about the education, training, and qualifications required for your chosen career.
- Study job specifications of interest.
- Discuss your goals with your loved ones.
- Approach school counselors, charities, and organizations to obtain advice.

CHILDREN IN THE U.S.

There are nearly 74 million children younger than age 18 in the United States, accounting for 23 percent of the total population.

POPULATION

The number of children in the country has grown since 1980, when there were 64 million children, and this number is projected to continue to increase to 80 million in 2050.

- **According to the National Center for Education Statistics, there are 98,817 public schools in the United States.** Source: Children's Bureau.

- **There are 34,576 private schools in the United States.** Source: Council for American Private Education.

- **On any given day, there are nearly 438,000 children in foster care in the United States.** Source: Children's Bureau.

CHILD ABUSE & NEGLECT FATALITIES

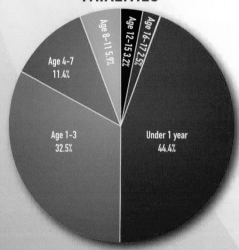

Age 16-17 2.5%

Age 12-15 3.2%

Age 8-11 5.9%

Age 4-7
11.4%

Age 1-3
32.5%

Under 1 year
44.4%

Source: Child Welfare Information Gateway.

POVERTY

- **About 15 million children in the United States—21% of all children—live in families with incomes below the federal poverty threshold.**

- **Poverty can impede children's ability to learn and contribute to social, emotional, and behavioral problems.**

- **Poverty also can contribute to poor physical and mental health.**
  Source: NCCP.

CHILD ABUSE

Research shows the youngest children are the most vulnerable to maltreatment. All states reported that most victims were younger than three years. The victimization rate was highest for children younger than one year of age.

- **Abused children are 25% more likely to experience teen pregnancy.**

- **The financial cost of child abuse and neglect in the United States is estimated at $585 billion.**

- **Abused teens are more likely to engage in sexual risk-taking behaviors, putting them at greater risk for STDs.**

- **About 30% of abused and neglected children will later abuse their own children, continuing the horrible cycle of abuse.**
  Source: American SPCC.

CHILD ABUSE

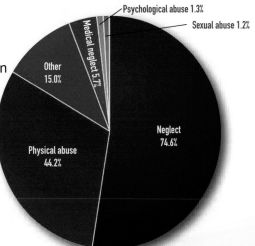

Psychological abuse 1.3%
Sexual abuse 1.2%
Medical neglect 5.7%
Other 15.0%
Neglect 74.6%
Physical abuse 44.2%

Source: Child Welfare Information Gateway.

DID YOU KNOW?

- **One child in every seven will be born into poverty in the United States.**

- **More than 13 million children in the United States live in "food insecure" homes.** Source: NCCP.

- **One out of six children—roughly 100 million—in developing countries is underweight.** Source: Food Aid Foundation.

- **World Food Program (WFP) calculates that US$3.2 billion is needed per year to reach all 66 million hungry school-age children.**

AWARENESS OF THE CAUSE

WHO HELPS CHILDREN IN NEED?

6 School
1 Police
5 Family
2 Charities
4 Helplines
3 Support Organizations

WHAT DO CHILDREN NEED FROM SOCIETY?

- Love
- Education
- Friendship
- Health care
- Emotional support

- Financial support
- Encouragement
- Play & mental stimulation
- Exercise
- Security

THE BENEFITS OF HELPING OTHERS

A SENSE OF PURPOSE

Giving to others provides a sense of purpose to an individual. People who volunteer for a cause feel that their life is worthwhile and satisfying. This ultimately leads to improved physical and emotional health.

EMOTIONAL HEALTH

Studies have also shown that the act of charity results in emotional well-being. The person who gives to charity feels improved self-esteem. This gives a feeling of satisfaction to the individual. In a way, giving to others allows the individual to create a "kindness bank account." The more kind acts are filled in the account, the better the emotional state of the person.

A HEALTHY HEART

A recent study found that there is a significant correlation between helping others and the heart's health. It was found that people who volunteer are about 40 percent less likely to develop high blood pressure as compared to those who do not volunteer.

HELPING OTHERS MAKES YOU HAPPY

According to research, people who engage in acts of kindness and giving are happier in general as compared to others. Acts of kindness carried out regularly or even once a week can lead to greater happiness and joy in life.

REDUCE STRESS

The act of helping others can also help reduce stress. Research shows that people who help others have lower cortisol levels. The presence of this hormone in the body causes it to create feelings of anxiety and panic, which can lead to higher blood pressure levels. People who do less for others have a higher level of the stress hormone in their body.

Milestone Moment

FORMATION OF AVID, 1980

In 1980, Mary Catherine Swanson was a teacher in an underserved area of San Diego. She noticed that many of her fellow teachers had low expectations for their students, and students tended to meet these expectations but reach no higher. Students were not living up to their full potential, and she wanted to make a change. Mrs. Swanson believed that if students were given higher expectations, they would rise to meet them.

Thus she created AVID: Advancement Via Individual Determination. The AVID system encourages teachers to teach students through higher-level thinking questions as opposed to simply asking them to memorize facts and dates. It also asserts that teachers should create a classroom culture that assumes children are going to college and provide students with academic, social, and emotional support that will help them succeed in education and life.

Today, AVID programs are active in more than 6,400 schools around the United States, affecting nearly 2 million students. The AVID program pushes pupils to do their best, and teachers learn how to help students reach their dreams, even when they come from neighborhoods and schools where they are not given the same advantages as their peers from higher-income neighborhoods.

The AVID system encourages children to live up to their full potential regardless of the neighborhood they live in.

WORDS TO UNDERSTAND

enrichment: an educational program that provides additional information or knowledge to students

intervention: in special education, modifications that help a student learn, such as preferential seating, frequent parent contact, having assignment directions read out loud, and so on

neglect: to pay little or no attention to, or to fail to care for something properly

reunification: in social work, the process of bringing separated parents and children back together

CHAPTER 2

Helping Children: Why It's Needed

WORKING WITH CHILDREN

From planning your day for preschool children as an early childhood educator, to helping children overcome trauma as a children's therapist, the options for careers working with children are nearly endless! All people who successfully work with children have a few things in common.

First, patience. Patience is required when working with kids. Young minds take more time to understand concepts than adult minds, and sometimes things need to be explained to kids in a variety of ways before ideas can begin to take hold. Patience is just as important when working with high school students as it is when working with very young children.

A DAY IN THE LIFE: EARLY CHILDHOOD TEACHER

An early childhood teacher arrives at their preschool or daycare center early in the morning so they can ensure that the classroom is ready for their little students. Many preschools and daycare facilities let parents drop children off before the school day begins, allowing them to get to work on time. This can mean very early mornings for early childhood teachers!

As children come into the classroom, teachers greet them and their parents. They typically check in with parents, asking how the child is doing, which gives the parents the opportunity to update them with any concerns or issues. As children come in the room, they're able to engage in free play as the teacher continues to welcome others coming in for the day. After all the students have arrived, it's time for morning meeting, when the teacher sings songs with the students, reads them stories, and talks about the topic of the week/month (weather, an upcoming holiday, animals, plants, etc.).

Morning meeting is typically followed by more free play, lunch, outdoor play, and a special activity, such as music or art. When children return to their classroom after their special, it's nap or quiet time. The teacher works to help all children settle for an hour or so, usually by playing soothing music and dimming the lights in the room.

After nap, it's outdoor time or free play until it's time for the children to go home. After the kids leave, the teacher spends some time planning for the next day and making parent phone calls if necessary. Being an early childhood teacher is a busy job, but it's incredibly rewarding to spend the day teaching little ones.

Second, a sense of humor! Working with children can be hysterical, and it's important to keep the sense of fun and wonder that comes with childhood, even on the frustrating days. Kids respond well to counselors, doctors, and teachers who are able to see the funny aspects of their job.

A career helping children is very rewarding. However, you will require many qualities including patience, a sense of humor and have a real interest in improving the lives of children.

Lastly, you must really, really enjoy children. Think about your school experience. Have you ever had a teacher who loved the subject they taught but didn't seem to care for the kids they were actually teaching? If you're going to spend the vast majority of your career interacting with kids or young adults, it's important that you truly enjoy working with that age group.

COUNSELOR

Many people think of adults as the only people with mental health issues, but children can have mental illnesses as well. About 20 percent of children in the United States suffer from some form of mental illness each year. A child counselor typically engages children in talk therapy, helping them through mental health issues, learning issues, and family problems. Child counselors work closely with parents and teachers, educating them on how they can best support the child.

A child counselor has many roles, but very often they typically help children by means of talk therapy.

Sometimes children refer themselves to a counselor, especially at school. When children are aware that a counselor is there in case they need to talk through a problem, they are likely to ask for counseling when they are struggling with social or emotional issues. Other times, teachers may refer struggling children to a counselor. Parents can also request counseling services for their child. Sometimes, children exhibit issues in the classroom that they do not show at home, and vice versa.

Children do not think or process events in the same way as adults, making it important for kids to have specialized counselors who understand the workings of a child's mind. Many counselors specialize in a certain area of mental wellness for children, such as supporting kids who struggle with attention deficit hyperactivity disorder (ADHD), obsessive compulsive disorder (OCD), or anxiety and/or depression. Counselors are not permitted to prescribe medication, but they may work with a child's doctor or psychiatrist if they believe that medication might be a positive support for the child. Child counselors may also work with parents to change the home environment if they believe that it may be contributing to a child's mental stressors.

FAMILY SUPPORT WORKER

Many families in the United States and Canada struggle to make ends meet financially and need help from federal and state resources. Some parents who need these services work multiple jobs and have a hard time finding the time to get through all of the paperwork required to apply for services. Family support workers help families determine if they're eligible for government support programs, such as food stamps, Medicaid, Medicare, and welfare. Helping families find out what they are eligible for before applying saves them time, since they know which programs are the best fit for their family and financial situation.

The rules for receiving aid from government programs are often complicated. Family support workers can help families fill out the extensive paperwork that they may need in order to receive government assistance. Family support workers may also be responsible for turning in paperwork to the state to prove that a family is eligible to receive aid.

While people in this career path need to have excellent knowledge of federal aid systems and organizational skills, they must also have a passion for helping children and their families get the resources that they need. Yes, this profession involves filling out paperwork and knowing a lot of rules. But family support workers are mainly there to help families get what they need and provide a sympathetic, understanding, nonjudgmental ear to parents and

A family support worker is there to provide a sympathetic, understanding, and nonjudgmental ear to parents and children who are having challenging times.

children who are going through a hard time. Coming forward and asking for help can be embarrassing for some families, and family support workers are there to make the process a little bit easier.

PLAY THERAPIST

When children are playing, they are doing so much more than just having fun! Play is how children learn, and play is also used to help children process their emotions. Play therapists work with children and their families, helping kids with trauma, behavioral issues, and family issues through the power of play.

A play therapist helps children with many challenging issues process their emotions through play.

There is a very specific science when it comes to play therapy. Play therapists use special techniques to elicit different responses from children. For example, to help a child process a traumatic experience, a play therapist may guide them through drawing a picture of the trauma or have them act out the trauma with dolls. It's important that this type of work is done only by a trained play therapist who knows how to use these techniques in a way that will not cause further damage to the child. This type of therapy should not be attempted by parents or teachers who have not been trained in how to use play to help children through trauma. Play therapy can be excellent for children who are especially shy or have been through many years of traumatic experiences.

SOCIAL WORKER

Social workers protect children and families that are vulnerable and in need of assistance. "Vulnerable" can mean many different things: being in poverty, struggling with addiction, having children with physical or behavioral disabilities, or going through a difficult time emotionally. Some social workers work for state agencies, some work in schools, and some work for hospitals. Much like family support workers, social workers help connect families with the federal and local resources that they need. Social workers are also trained to diagnose and treat mental, emotional, and behavioral issues.

While social workers usually work full-time, they may also be needed to work on evenings and during weekends. A social worker's job can be intensely emotional,

A social worker's role is to provide much needed assistance to vulnerable families. Social workers always do their best to keep families together.

especially when they have to make the difficult decision that a child needs to be removed from their family home and placed into foster care. Social workers always do their best to keep families together, and when that isn't possible, they develop a plan for family **reunification** down the road.

EARLY CHILDHOOD TEACHER

If you enjoy working with very young children, becoming an early childhood educator might be a good fit for you. The science of early childhood education is different from the science of educating older children. Many things that come simply to adults, such as finding patterns, hearing specific sounds in words, and putting things in order, are brand-new skills for young children.

Early childhood teachers typically are employed by preschools and daycare centers, providing education to the littlest learners. They may work with newborn infants, all the way up to children who are almost ready to start kindergarten. Skills taught by early childhood educators can range from learning colors to learning to read simple words. Class sizes are usually small at this age, allowing teachers to spend plenty of time interacting with children one on one.

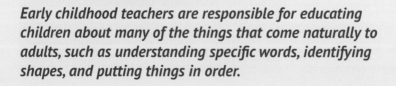

Unlike middle and high school, early childhood teachers are typically with the same children for the entire school day, from the moment they come

Early childhood teachers are responsible for educating children about many of the things that come naturally to adults, such as understanding specific words, identifying shapes, and putting things in order.

Working with very young children is an important job. A good early education will benefit a child's learning abilities, so when they begin kindergarten, they get a head start.

in the classroom to hang up their coats until the moment their parents pick them up. This gives early childhood teachers the chance to work with their kids in a variety of settings, from classrooms to outdoor play to lunch.

CHILD PSYCHOLOGIST

Child psychologists help children through emotional, social, and mental difficulties. Some child psychologists also work with children who have been through trauma. A psychologist is a doctor, but they are not permitted to prescribe medicine. Child psychologists may work with a team—including doctors, nurses, and

Autism spectrum disorders (ASD) are treated by a number of health professionals including psychologists, mental health specialists, and pediatricians.

psychiatrists—that collaborates to figure out the best course of treatment for a child who is suffering from a mental illness.

While child psychologists often work with children with severe emotional disturbances, they can also assist children who have minor issues, such as shyness or dyslexia. Some parents think that they should seek the help of a child psychologist only when their child is suffering from a major problem, but psychologists can be helpful to a child coping with a variety of situations, such as divorce, moving to a new town, and dealing with social issues at school. Some child psychologists work in hospitals, but many are also employed by schools. In some school districts, there is one child psychologist that rotates between a few different schools, serving hundreds of children at once.

Child psychologists often work with children with severe emotional disturbances. It is a highly skilled and demanding role.

ESOL TEACHER

ESOL stands for "English for Speakers of Other Languages." ESOL teachers work with students who did not grow up speaking English as their primary language at home. While it is helpful for ESOL teachers to be fluent in the primary language of the children they teach, it is not necessary. Many ESOL teachers work in areas where there is a high concentration of immigrants from countries that do not primarily speak English.

In some schools, ESOL teachers only teach English to students. In other schools, especially school districts with larger populations of students who do not speak English, there may be a full ESOL department in which all of the teachers are ESOL trained and all of the students are in the process of learning English. Teaching ESOL students presents many challenges, especially when it comes to communicating with parents about their child's progress.

ESOL teachers have an interesting role. They usually work in school districts with larger populations of students who do not speak English.

Many ESOL teachers find that they especially enjoy teaching math to their students, as numbers and mathematics are a language that is easily understood between all parties involved. While teaching English is a primary component to ESOL, many teachers also explain about American and Canadian cultural concepts as well, including holidays, foods, customs, and slang.

LEARNING MENTOR

Are you interested in teaching students, but not interested in spending your days in a school? Becoming a learning mentor might be a good fit for you. Learning mentors typically work in after-school tutoring centers, providing

Learning mentors typically work in after-school tutoring centers, providing extra tutoring for those who need it.

enrichment education or additional help to students who need it. Most learning mentor positions are part-time, and they are often filled by high school or college students who are interested in eventually working with children in a full-time career. Learning mentors may help students in all subjects, or they may specialize in a specific subject, such as math or science. Some learning mentors work at after-school programs that provide general enrichment to students outside of school hours.

THERAPEUTIC STAFF SUPPORT WORKER

Therapeutic staff support workers, or TSS workers, are adults who are assigned to help one particular student during their school day. A TSS worker travels throughout the school during the day with the child, accompanying them to their classes, lunch, and recess. The level of involvement depends on the needs of the child. For some children, their TSS worker will sit next to them in each class, helping them participate in the class and complete their assignments. For other children, the TSS worker may sit in the back of the room, only stepping in to help the child when necessary.

TSS workers are assigned to students who have autism, attention deficit hyperactivity disorder, emotional disturbances, and learning disabilities. A TSS worker is able to provide the student with one-on-one support—the individual attention they need—while they can still participate in a regular classroom setting. Schools in the United States and Canada have the goal of including all students in regular education whenever it's possible, and TSS workers are an important part of that goal.

A TSS worker is able to provide a child with one-on-one support, thus allowing the child to still participate in a regular classroom setting.

ELEMENTARY TEACHER

An elementary school teacher works with students in kindergarten through grades 5 or 6, depending on the school. Most elementary school teachers teach reading, math, language arts, social studies, and science to their pupils. In some schools, elementary students switch classes for subjects. In these schools, teachers may teach only one or two subjects. Specialized teachers come into the classroom on a weekly basis to teach art, music, physical education, and health.

It may seem like elementary school teachers have an easy job, but nothing could be further from the truth. Teaching an entire classroom of young children reading, writing, and math skills is incredibly difficult—and incredibly important. Most elementary school teachers work far more hours than what they're paid for each week, putting in extra time before and/or after school and on the weekends to make sure their classroom and lessons are ready for their kids.

An elementary teacher works with kindergarten students through grades 5 or 6, depending on the school.

HIGH SCHOOL TEACHER

High school teachers have a different day-to-day schedule than teachers of younger children. Typically, high school teachers specialize in one subject area, but they may teach more than one subject within that area. For example, a science teacher might teach both biology and chemistry. Depending on their assigned schedule, a high school teacher might teach the same class four to seven times per day to different groups of students.

During their free periods during the day, teachers tutor

A high school teacher is a demanding role. They must often work beyond the normal hours for which they are paid.

students, grade papers, and plan upcoming lessons. While this sounds like it could get repetitive, high school teachers are quick to say that it's anything but. Each new group of students throughout the day brings new questions, ideas, and challenges. Much like elementary school teachers, high school teachers work far beyond the hours for which they are paid.

SCHOOL AIDE

A school aide is a helper to teachers, administrators, and staff. Aides are most common in elementary schools, where they are typically assigned to specific teachers. A teacher may request to have an aide in the classroom when they're doing a science experiment or a special craft. Aides may also work with specific groups of students after students have been given different assignments based on their academic level.

Working as a classroom aide is a great way to get exposed to different teaching styles. Some aides also help with general needs around the school, such as supervising children during pickup, drop-off, lunch, and recess.

SPECIAL-NEEDS TEACHER

Special-needs teachers work with students who have behavioral, emotional, and learning differences that require a different approach to learning than a typical student. Some special-needs teachers provide in-classroom support in regular education classrooms, and others teach in self-contained classrooms. Being a special education teacher requires lots of knowledge about how to meet the needs of students with learning differences. Most special-needs teachers work with students who have a variety of needs, rather than working with only one type of learning need.

School aides help with the general needs around the school including helping teachers, administrators, and other staff.

Special-needs teachers require lots of knowledge as the students in their care may have a variety of complex needs.

Special-needs teachers are also responsible for creating Individualized Education Plans (also known as IEPs) for special-needs students. These plans dictate how instruction needs to be modified for these students throughout the school. Parents, administrators, and other teachers all have input on IEPs, and the special education teacher is looked to as the expert on the **interventions** necessary to meet the needs of the student.

SPEECH-LANGUAGE PATHOLOGIST

A speech-language pathologist is a specialist who works with children with a variety of speech disorders. These disorders may be mild, such as delayed speech, or more serious, such as speech disorders caused by autism or Down syndrome. Speech-language pathologists teach children skills that help them speak, and communicate with others.

There are many special techniques that speech-language pathologists use to help children learn how to speak, including modeling speech, listening to recordings, and helping children to imitate certain sounds. Some speech-language pathologists are even trained to help teach children how to swallow and eat, as eating problems are often associated with speech issues. A speech-language pathologist can be vital in helping a child learn how to speak properly, which will allow their confidence and social skills to skyrocket in the classroom.

PEDIATRICIAN

A pediatrician is a doctor who specializes in the medical treatment of children, ranging from newborn to age twenty-one. Most pediatricians see children for routine physical care, such as checkups and treatment for simple illnesses. These medical doctors are trained to treat behavioral, emotional, and social health as well. Pediatricians track children's growth, development, and improvement or decline in any chronic health conditions. Pediatricians work closely with parents in helping them address any issues that they child may have.

Most pediatricians are general doctors who treat all aspects of children's well-being. Some specialize in certain areas, such as helping children who have neurological issues or helping children who have cancer. Pediatricians

Speech-language pathologists help children with a variety of speech disorders including some more serious speech disorders associated with autism or Down syndrome.

spend the majority of their time providing direct patient care, but they also must spend time completing patient paperwork, calling parents for follow-ups, and updating nurses on patient care needs.

CHILD WELFARE SPECIALIST

Child welfare specialists are also known as child protective service specialists. These government employees provide counseling, case management, assessment, and social services to families. Child welfare specialists work to help parents and guardians take care of their children in

Pediatricians are doctors who specialize in all aspects of a child's well-being.

the best way. Child welfare specialists are frequently called into help families that are deemed high risk by the children's school. These workers also refer parents and guardians to community services that may be of use for their family.

Child welfare specialists are heavily involved in adoption and foster care placements. Most child welfare specialists work closely with social workers, aiding in the reunification process between parents and children whenever possible. Being a child welfare specialist can be extremely emotionally difficult work, especially when the job involves separating a child from a parent.

SCHOOL COUNSELOR

School counselors help students with a variety of issues, from problems at home to deciding which college to attend. School counselors can also help with academic issues, such as helping students maintain their focus in class and helping them make sure they remember to get their homework done. Some school counseling offices have an open door policy, allowing students to come talk to a counselor at any time.

Certain teenage issues may seem insignificant to some adults (such as popularity issues, bullying, and health concerns), but counselors know that these issues can mean everything to students. School counselors take their concerns

Child welfare specialists help children who are at high risk. Their job can be extremely emotionally difficult especially when it involves young children who have been abused.

School counselors help students with a variety of problems that may occur at home or at school. A counselor will always take a student's concerns seriously.

seriously, and they help students to work through their issues in a productive and healthy way. Some school counselors also teach classes on topics such as mental, emotional, and social health.

These professionals also work with parents to help them learn the best ways to help their children navigate the everyday issues of life at school. Some school counselors run group therapy sessions for students who are dealing with similar issues.

WHAT'S A MANDATED REPORTER?

Mandated reporters include teachers, social workers, mental health professionals, childcare workers, law enforcement officials, and other people who work with children on a regular basis. Mandated reporters are required by law to report suspected child abuse or neglect to the relevant authorities in their state. While the laws surrounding mandated reporting differ slightly from state to state, the basic idea is the same. In the majority of states, reports that are made are kept anonymous—the reporter's name is not shared with the person suspected of child abuse or neglect—and there are no repercussions for someone accidentally making a false report.

Mandated reporters are by no means investigators. If they suspect abuse or neglect, it is their job simply to report the issue. From there, professional investigators will find out whether or not there is an issue to be handled.

EARLY CHILDHOOD EDUCATION

Learn more about what it's like to major in early childhood education

TEXT-DEPENDENT QUESTIONS

1. What's one task that a social worker might have in a typical day?

2. What does a family support specialist do?

3. What's one way that teaching early childhood education is different from teaching elementary school?

RESEARCH PROJECT

Interview someone who has one of the jobs mentioned in this chapter. Find out what their college major was, and ask them if they feel that they were fully prepared for their job when they started. Ask them what their favorite part of their job is, and to describe a typical day at work.

CHILD ABUSE PREVENTION AND TREATMENT ACT (CAPTA), 1974

CAPTA is a piece of legislation that works to keep children safe.

Passed in 1974 and revamped in 2010, CAPTA is the largest piece of legislation in the United States that works to keep children safe. There are many different facets to this legislation. One part is mandatory reporting laws. These laws require people who work with children in an official capacity (teachers, pediatricians, counselors) to report suspected child abuse to government officials so that the child can be kept safe. CAPTA also gives money to communities to aid their efforts in stopping child abuse and neglect. This allows local governments to hire social workers and counselors to work to keep the community's children safe.

Lastly, the legislation also provides support to communities in caring for abandoned infants. Sometimes infants are born to families who are unable to care for them, often due to drug addiction. This legislation provides communities with funding to help rehabilitate these families so that they are able to care for their children and for foster families to support children in the meantime.

WORDS TO UNDERSTAND

altruistic: the act of giving and expecting nothing in return; someone who helps others without expecting payment, such as a volunteer

rehabilitate: to restore to a former state; to help a person get back to normal life after illness or addiction

work-study: a college student program that is a cross between volunteering and being employed; often part of a financial aid package that allows students to earn money (and potentially course credits) for working a job within the college or university

CHAPTER **3**

Volunteering and Organizations

VOLUNTEERING

If you think you might be interested in working with children as a long-term career, it's important to get some volunteer experience first. There are many different opportunities for working with children, from reading in preschools to being a babysitter. If you're volunteering, you may be able to earn credit toward your senior project community service hours for your school.

Remember, as a volunteer, patience is critical. It will take children some time to warm up to you, and that does not mean that you are doing anything wrong. Children need to see you a few times in their classroom or home before they begin to feel comfortable interacting with you. This is completely normal! Getting used to the warming-up period is great practice if you decide to become a teacher or counselor one day. Over time, you'll learn different techniques that work for your personality in helping kids get comfortable with you.

While you may not be considered a mandated reporter as a volunteer, it's important to report any suspected neglect or child abuse to your supervisor. Even if you aren't quite sure whether or not something negative is happening to the child, err on the side of caution and let your supervisor make that call. It's always better to report it if you are unsure. During your volunteer training, be sure that you know what to do and/or who to contact in case you have something you feel you need to report.

Helping children by volunteering is a worthwhile and rewarding experience. It will also help you decide on the kind of career you may choose in the future.

AMERICA READS

This organization teaches college students how to provide reading education to children at preschool and daycare centers. Typically, college students volunteer with this program as part of a **work-study** opportunity offered by their college or university. Before being placed with a preschool or daycare center, America Reads participants take a class instructing them on proper techniques for reading to children. While simply reading a book may seem easy, it can actually be quite a task to get little ones to pay attention!

The class teaches readers how to ask questions that keep children engaged, what are the appropriate book lengths for different ages, and how

As a volunteer for America Reads, you assist a preschool teacher by reading to children and encouraging them to become interested in books and reading.

to read in an engaging tone that makes children curious about what is going to happen next. As an America Reads volunteer, you'll go to a preschool classroom a few times a week, assisting the teacher, reading to children, and helping to supervise daily activities.

RELIGIOUS ORGANIZATIONS

If you belong to a religious organization such as a church or synagogue, it may be a good place to get started working with children. Most religious organizations offer childcare for parents who want to attend services. There is almost always a need for childcare workers, which will allow you to have a short time (usually sixty minutes or less) working with children.

Some religious organizations also have children's programs in which you can volunteer to provide children with religious education during the time their parents are attending the service. This can be a great way to get a feel for whether or not you would like to be a teacher one day. It is also a perfect chance to earn community service hours for a senior project at school.

A DAY IN THE LIFE: PEDIATRICIAN

A pediatrician's hours can look different depending on where they work. For a pediatrician who works in private practice, they may be able to set their own hours and/or schedule their own appointments. For a pediatrician who works in a hospital, their schedule can be different depending on their specialty or the department in which they work. When a pediatrician starts their shift, they check in with nurses to see if there are any pressing needs. In inpatient units (areas of the hospital in which patients are admitted and not just coming for an appointment), pediatricians will make rounds—this means that they check on each patient and see how they are doing. After making rounds, they'll spend more time with patients who need additional care, perform tests, prescribe medications, and perhaps even get opinions from other doctors on the best course of treatment for their patients.

Pediatricians in outpatient units spend their days seeing patients for appointments. Most pediatricians in outpatient units see a mix of patients who are sick and who are coming in for checkups. Pediatricians may specialize in caring for a certain age, or they may see children of all ages. An important part of a pediatrician's day is also calling patients who were recently seen or who are adjusting to a new medication to see how they are doing.

BIG BROTHERS, BIG SISTERS (BBBS)

BBBS is an organization that provides an adult as a role model, confidante, and friend to children who need one. Some children who are involved in BBBS are from families who are struggling financially. Others are from single-parent homes, and some simply need an additional positive influence in their lives. You need to be eighteen in order to be an official big brother or sister.

Sometimes students are referred to BBBS by their school counselor; other times they are referred by teachers or their parents. As a "Big," you'll be screened by a match specialist on your interests and gender (most of the time, Big Brothers are paired with boys, Big Sisters are paired with girls) who will then find a "Little" for you. You and your Little will participate in **altruistic** events that the organization runs, and you'll also have the opportunity to take your Little on outings, just the two of you.

It's up to you whether you'd like to do a school-based or community-based match. In school-based matches, you'll go to the child's school, enjoying lunch, recess, or classroom time with them. In community-based matches, you'll meet outside of the school day. As a Big, you'll communicate regularly with the child's parent or guardian, staying aware of any needs or issues happening in their lives.

BBBS is well worth volunteering for. You will be helping children who may have many challenges in their lives.

WOMEN'S SHELTERS

In most cities, there are shelters that focus on women who are in need of housing due to leaving abusive relationships. Often, these women are mothers who are doing their best to keep their children safe. In leaving their relationship, they often find themselves without a vehicle, employment, or housing.

Volunteering at a women's shelter can include a lot of work with children, specifically, keeping kids occupied and happy while their moms receive training, counseling, work on résumés, and go out for job interviews. Knowing that their children are occupied, safe, and having fun helps moms do their best when working to get their lives back on track.

Children who live at women's shelters are often going through difficult times. A volunteer's work can include keeping kids occupied while their moms receive counseling.

RONALD MCDONALD HOUSE CHARITIES

The Ronald McDonald House Charities organization provides housing to families who have a child needing medical treatment at a hospital that is far away from their home. Ronald McDonald Houses allow parents to stay near the hospital where their child is receiving treatment at little or no cost. The facility provides private bedrooms, home-cooked meals, and playrooms for the siblings of the child who is receiving treatment, with several families sharing the house. Families are asked to make a payment of $25 per day, but if they are

Ronald McDonald Houses provide low- or no-cost accommodation (similar to the room above) to the parents and other siblings of a child receiving treatment at a nearby hospital.

unable to afford this payment, it is waived. No family is ever turned away for their inability to pay.

There are many different volunteer opportunities at Ronald McDonald Houses. Volunteers may be asked to take on various roles depending on the needs of the families staying in the house. Responsibilities may include cooking, cleaning, talking to families who are having a hard time, escorting families to the correct wing of the hospital, playing with the siblings of the child receiving treatment in the house's play area, and yardwork and/or playground upkeep.

ORGANIZATIONS

CITY YEAR

City Year places college graduate volunteers in underserved schools in urban areas. City Year helpers serve as classroom aides, student mentors, and tutors to students. This is a fantastic opportunity for young adults who have finished college and aren't quite sure what they'd like to do next but know that they want to make an impact on the world. City Year volunteers often go on to become teachers.

Studies have shown that schools in low-income areas are often understaffed, and students need additional support to realize their potential. Many schools in these areas have extremely large class sizes (thirty-plus students in a single class), and teachers need help in order to reach all of their students with differing ability levels and academic needs.

City Year volunteers serve as classroom aides, student mentors, and tutors to students in underserved schools in urban areas.

A certified Red Cross babysitter allows a young person to look after children. It's a great way of gaining work experience.

RED CROSS

One of the best ways to gain experience working with children is through providing babysitting services. The Red Cross offers a babysitting certification course that is essential for young babysitters. In the class, you'll learn how to give CPR in case of an emergency, different ways to entertain young children, and how to use positive reinforcement to help children be on their best behavior.

When advertising your babysitting business to potential customers, be sure to mention that you're certified by the Red Cross. Parents will feel more comfortable allowing you to watch their children when they know that a trusted organization has given you the thumbs-up.

GIRLS ON THE RUN (GOTR)

If you're athletic, GOTR could be a perfect volunteer experience for you! This organization helps girls enhance their self-esteem while training to run a 5K race and teaches life skills through dynamic, conversation-based lessons and running games. GOTR leaders help girls make running fun while also teaching weekly lessons on health, self-esteem, and positivity. Running is naturally integrated into these weekly lessons, so the girls learn to see running—or any kind of exercise—as a fun part of everyday life, not something boring or tedious that they have to do to stay fit.

GOTR leaders lead these weekly practices and eventually run a 5K race with their girls. Even if you aren't able to make the commitment to be a GOTR leader, the organization is also always looking for female volunteers to run with girls in their first 5K. For an experienced runner, a 5K might not feel like a big deal, but for a girl who has never run a race before, it can be a scary experience! Running buddies stay with their assigned girl throughout the race, encouraging them to keep going, and helping them get to the finish line, even if they need to take walking breaks.

SPECIAL OLYMPICS

Are you interested in sports and helping kids with disabilities? Volunteering with the Special Olympics could be a great fit for you! The Special Olympics is the world's largest sports organization for adults and kids with disabilities, and they have many different volunteer opportunities available. Some volunteers spend many hours each week working with athletes, while

Girls on the Run volunteers help girls make running fun while also teaching them lessons in health, self-esteem, and positivity.

The Special Olympics is always in need of volunteers who can help children and adults.

others volunteer only during the Special Olympics World Games, which occur every two years.

The Special Olympics welcomes volunteers of all ages, from young children to adults. If you're thinking about becoming a teacher or therapist for children with special needs, volunteering with the Special Olympics is an excellent way to see if this is a good career path for you.

Special Olympics
WORLD
GAMES

ASSISTANCE DOGS

Many children and adults with disabilities depend on assistance dogs to help them complete their daily activities, such as retrieving dropped items, opening and closing doors, and even going for a walk. Assistance dogs undergo intensive training before they are matched with an owner. There are many organizations that train dogs that will eventually become assistance dogs, and these organizations often accept volunteers.

Assistance Dogs International (ADI) welcomes volunteers to its organization. This can ultimately lead to a job as a qualified trainer. Founded in 1986, ADI has become a leading authority in the assistance dog field. The organization specializes in all aspects of assistance dog acquisition, training, and partnership.

SPECIAL OLYMPICS

Get a firsthand look at what it's like to volunteer for the Special Olympics

TEXT-DEPENDENT QUESTIONS

1. What's one thing babysitters learn while taking the Red Cross Babysitting certification course?

2. Why might a college senior decide to apply to volunteer with City Year?

3. What's one task that a volunteer might have at a women's shelter?

RESEARCH PROJECT

Spend a day volunteering with one of the organizations listed above or with another organization in your area that serves the needs of children. Report on how the experience went. What's something you learned? What was different than you expected? How did the volunteer experience shape your thoughts about your potential career working with children?

Milestone Moment

PASSAGE OF THE FAIR LABOR STANDARDS ACT, 1938

It's hard to imagine, but less than a century ago, many children were working seventy-hour workweeks in factories, mines, and other unsafe places. There were no laws to protect these children, and it was not mandatory that they be in school. Many kids were hurt performing jobs that should have been done by adults.

In 1938, the Fair Labor Standards Act was passed. You have probably heard of these referred to as "child labor laws." These laws protect children and mandate the hours they are permitted to work. While each state and/or province in the United States and Canada has its own specific rules, generally, children under fourteen are permitted to work only on a very limited basis (selling homemade goods, delivering newspapers, babysitting, acting, etc.). There are specific regulations that prohibit children from performing dangerous jobs, such as mining. While child labor laws are not perfect in the United States and Canada, they have come a long way in the past 100 years toward protecting children.

The Fair Labor Standards Act protects children from being exploited in the workplace.

CHAPTER 4

Education, Training, and Qualifications

EDUCATION

If you're interested in working with children, you'll need to undergo some specialized training, no matter what type of job you pursue. Most jobs in this career field require employees to get continuing education credits throughout their career. These credits are earned by taking classes that teach the latest techniques in the field and can include new teaching techniques, learning about new research in the field, or becoming certified in a new area. Often, employers will pay for these credits. Many people who work with children are able to use continuing education credits to earn graduate degrees, all while fulfilling the educational requirements for their job.

HIGH SCHOOL GRADUATE

There are many jobs for high school graduates in the field of helping children. Some people work at this level while studying for their bachelor's

Learning mentor programs provide valuable experience to students who are interested in working with children.

degree. This is a great idea for two reasons: it can help to offset the cost of a college education, and it offers valuable field experience.

Learning mentor programs frequently hire high-achieving students who are still in high school. If you're interested in working with children but do not yet have your high school diploma, working as a learning mentor can be a fantastic place to start! After-school learning mentorship programs typically have flexible hours, and you may even be able to count your hours there as class credit at school.

Daycare centers and preschools employ assistant teachers who have high school diplomas. Many of these jobs look for a Child Development Associate certificate, or CDA. A CDA certificate is earned in a child development course taken while in high school. Earning a CDA is a lot of hard work, but it's worth it if you want to work with children after you graduate from high school!

The CDA program involves a few different components. First you'll take classes in child development at your school. Then you'll get some practical, hands-on experience working at a preschool or daycare facility as part of your studies. You won't get paid for this work, but you'll earn class credit.

Having this certificate will make it much more likely that you'll be hired in a daycare or preschool immediately after high school before pursuing additional schooling.

In some schools, teachers' aides are not required to have a completed bachelor's degree. Working as an aide is a terrific position for someone who has graduated from high school but has yet to finish their college degree. Watching an experienced teacher succeed in the classroom can give you a lot of ideas for how you'd like to run your own classroom one day. If you're interested in becoming a teacher, let the teacher who you work with know! They may be able to give you tips and tricks that you won't learn in school.

When you excel as a teacher's aide, the school administrators tend to take notice. Your good performance could lead to an eventual job offer after you finish your bachelor's degree.

TSS workers are required to have a high school diploma as well. Many special-education majors take jobs as TSS workers while they are pursuing their bachelor's degree. While giving 100 percent attention to one student is a lot of work, many TSS workers report an extreme sense of satisfaction from watching their student grow over time.

Being employed as a TSS worker is an excellent experience that will help you learn how important it is for special-education teachers to cater to the needs of each student, applying interventions as necessary to help them succeed.

Many after-school programs have job openings for high school graduates. Often, these jobs are

Learning support staff can include teachers' aides, after-school mentors, assistant teachers, after-school program workers, and TSS workers.

A DAY IN THE LIFE: PLAY THERAPIST

Some play therapists work in private practice and set their own hours, while others work for large organizations, such as hospitals and schools. A play therapist's day typically consists of appointments to conduct play therapy with children. Some of these appointments may be one on one with a child—especially for play therapists who work in schools. Other appointments may involve one or both of the children's parents.

Some play therapists work as needed at police stations, helping children talk about the trauma they have experienced. While being a play therapist can be a lot of fun, it can also be emotionally challenging to support children through difficult experiences.

part-time, and they are a great way to get some experience working with children while you are still in school. The responsibilities of working at an after-school program can involve planning activities for children, communicating with parents, helping children with homework, and helping children complete educational projects.

If you decide to work immediately after high school, your employer may be willing to help you pay for your bachelor's degree while you work for their facility. Some employers who do this require you to sign a contract stating that you will continue to work there while earning your degree and/or for a number of years after your degree is complete. Other employers have arrangements to provide an employee with a set amount of money in addition to your usual pay for each year that you're enrolled in school at least half-time. If you want to pursue higher education but can't afford it immediately after high school, talk to your employer to find out if they offer tuition assistance.

BACHELOR'S DEGREE

Most jobs that involve helping children require a bachelor's degree. All teachers and school administrators are required to have at college education with a minimum of a bachelor's degree. Above that, the type of degree required will depend on the position.

For example, different education degrees allow teachers to teach different subjects and grade levels. Just like jobs at the high school graduate level, jobs at the bachelor's level will also require employees to complete continuing education courses to ensure that their knowledge is up to date.

While earning a bachelor's degree in education, college students are required to get practical, hands-on experience as student teachers. A student teaching assignment usually takes a full year. In the first semester of the year, the students observe teachers in different subject and grade-level areas. They may also visit schools of different **affluency levels**.

In the second semester of student teaching, the students teach one or more classes while being observed by the classroom teacher. This semester is typically a lot of work, as the student is likely also meeting with their peers to discuss classroom experiences and checking in with their faculty advisor. Student teaching can open a new teacher's eyes to what it takes to be successful in the classroom.

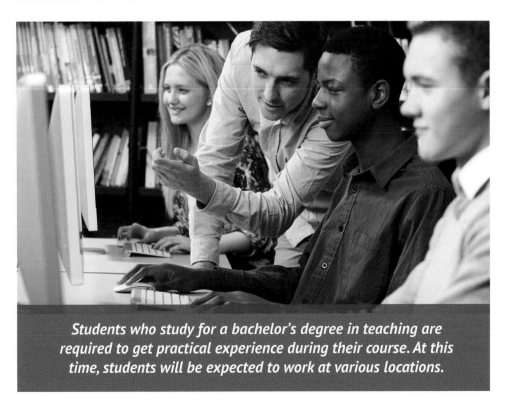

Students who study for a bachelor's degree in teaching are required to get practical experience during their course. At this time, students will be expected to work at various locations.

Many other jobs in schools—such as the dean, an administrator, and learning support staff—require bachelor's degrees as well.

Deans

A dean is the discipline expert in a school. In some schools, counselors, assistant principals, and the principal may take on the role of the dean. When the position exists, deans step in to help teachers, students, and parents with behavioral issues in and out of the classroom.

Administrators

This job level includes principals, vice-principals, division heads, and department heads. These professionals may also teach classes while taking care of their administrative duties, which can include conducting professional development for staff, observing and critiquing teachers, and organizing student schedules.

Learning Support Staff

As discussed, teachers' aides, after-school learning mentors, assistant teachers, after-school program workers, and TSS workers fall under the category of learning support staff.

GRADUATE DEGREE

Some jobs working with children require a graduate degree. A graduate degree is

Administrators are responsible for the smooth running of an organization. They may be responsible for acquiring staff and dealing with funding. They may also teach classes.

earned after earning a four-year undergraduate bachelor's degree. Graduate degrees include a medical doctor's degree (MD), a psychiatrist's degree (MD), a doctor of philosophy degree (PhD), and a master's degree (MEd or MS). Most professionals who are in the process of earning their graduate degree are also working full- or part-time in a school or at a university, teaching classes to undergraduate students.

Counselors, therapists, and psychologists all require graduate degrees. Counselors and therapists both require at least a master's degree. A master's degree is completed with a two- or three-year course of study. One of these years is spent completing an internship and practicum hours when students observe other mental health professionals at work in a school, hospital, or counseling office. After months of observation and training, they take on clients of their own. They meet regularly with their supervisor to discuss therapeutic techniques and receive critique about their work and ways they can improve their skills.

To become a pediatrician, students must first acquire an undergraduate degree, then study at medical school, and finally complete a residency.

For all jobs working with children and other vulnerable groups, applicants have to pass a background check. It is rare that a person can be hired with a criminal record.

Social workers, family support workers, and child protection services workers are all also required to have at least a master's degree. While these jobs require many classes, there is no substitute for on-the-job training, especially when dealing with traumatic and other difficult situations involving children and their families. A graduate-level social work program prepares social workers to be able to face these challenges day in and day out.

Psychiatrists and pediatricians are medical doctors who must complete medical school before they are able to practice. While the exact time line can vary depending on the program and the amount of courses the student takes at one time, it typically takes eight years (after getting a four-year undergraduate degree) to finish medical school. At least three years of medical school are spent completing a residency. During residency, the doctor-in-training sees patients while under the supervision of a more experienced doctor. After their residency, doctors must take a series of difficult tests in order to be licensed by the state in which they practice.

TRAINING AND QUALIFICATIONS

While education can provide a lot of knowledge and experience, on-the-job training is vital when it comes to working with kids. There is no amount of reading or classwork that can take the place of working with kids face-to-face. One thing that helps children thrive is routine, so all organizations, businesses, and facilities that take care of children have their own routines in place. When you get a job working in these locations, it will take some time to get to know the routine of your workplace. This is all a part of training, and it doesn't take long to catch on.

For any job working with children, a potential employee must submit to a background check. Having issues on a background check will often make it very difficult to be hired to work with children. People working with children must also be fingerprinted so that their fingerprints are in a national registry and can be checked to see if they are already in that national registry. It is very rare that an organization that works with children will hire someone with a criminal record.

Many professional jobs working with children require the passage of special state tests. Teachers, for instance, must take a variety of tests that are called "the Praxis" in combination. The Praxis 1 consists of reading, writing, and math sections and is similar to the SAT tests. The Praxis 2 is a more involved test that is specific to a teacher's specialty area, such as elementary education, biology, or secondary English. Most teachers find that the Praxis 2 is much more difficult than the Praxis 1.

In some high-need areas, teachers can be hired with only an emergency certification. This means that they have not completed their teacher training and may have yet to pass their Praxis. In most states, teachers are allowed to work for two years with an emergency certification. This certification is most commonly used in urban and rural areas for subjects that have a shortage of teachers, such as math and science.

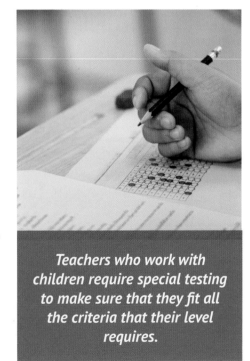

Teachers who work with children require special testing to make sure that they fit all the criteria that their level requires.

HOW DO I KNOW WHICH AGE GROUP I WANT TO ASSIST?

If you're interested in working with children, it can be difficult to figure out which age you'd like to work with, and this is where volunteering comes in. It's a good idea to have volunteer positions that focus on different age levels. You may be surprised to find that you really enjoy working with older students, or that the newborn room at the daycare facility is where you prefer spending your time!

Give yourself plenty of opportunities to explore all age groups before you choose a college major and commit to working with kids in one age group.

CHILD DEVELOPMENT ASSOCIATE CERTIFICATE

Learn more about how earning a Child Development Associate certificate can help kick-start your career working with children

TEXT-DEPENDENT QUESTIONS

1. What is one job working with children for which you need to obtain a bachelor's degree?

2. If you want to become a pediatrician, what type of degree do you need to earn?

3. What are continuing education credits?

RESEARCH PROJECT

Choose a local college or university, and research their education programs. What specialties do they offer? How much does the program cost? What does the student teaching year entail? Based on your research, does it sound like a program that interests you? Why or why not?

Milestone Moment

INDIVIDUALS WITH DISABILITIES EDUCATION ACT, 2004

The Individuals with Disabilities Education Act ensures that all children with special needs have the opportunity to obtain an appropriate education. This act requires public schools to provide individualized education to students with disabilities at no additional cost to the student's family. It also requires the school to evaluate the student's needs and then meet them in the least restrictive way, including the student in regular education classes (with modifications for the student when necessary) whenever possible.

This act also requires the school to involve both the student and the parent in the process of creating the student's Individualized Education Plan. When students and parents are both invested and have a say in the educational process, the student is more likely to succeed.

This important act requires public schools to provide special-needs students individualized education.

autonomy: independence, the ability to make one's own rules

bilingual: a person's ability to speak two languages fluently

negotiating: the process of obtaining or bringing about a desired outcome (such as a new salary)

CHAPTER 5

Salaries, Job Outlook, and Work Satisfaction

CAREERS AND SALARIES

If you're considering a career with children, it's important to make sure you choose a path that will help you earn a salary that you feel comfortable with. The numbers listed here are averages. Areas with a higher cost of living (such as in or near a large city) will likely pay higher salaries, while rural areas with a lower cost of living are more likely to pay lower salaries.

With any career, it's possible to ask for more than what you are offered in the beginning stages of getting a job. **Negotiating** is common, and it's easier to negotiate a higher salary when you have a resume packed with volunteer experiences and top-notch letters of recommendation from prior supervisors and volunteer coordinators.

A DAY IN THE LIFE: HIGH SCHOOL TEACHER

It's easy to think that high school teachers simply teach classes, but there is a lot of work that goes on behind the scenes! Teachers typically arrive at school much earlier than their students to get the classroom ready for the day. In addition to teaching classes, teachers also work with students one-on-one, often before and after school. During their one or two preparation periods during the day, teachers meet with administrators, grade student work, create assignments for students, plan lessons, make phone calls to update parents on their child's progress, talk with coaches about the academic eligibility for their student athletes, work with their subject and grade teams to discuss new best practices on how to reach their students, and talk with counselors about student needs.

If this sounds like a lot of work, it is! Many teachers end up needing much more time than the hour or two they get during the day to fully prepare to do their job well. Most end up staying for an extra one to two hours at the end of the school day, as well as doing some work on the weekends. Lots of high school teachers also coach a sport as a way to spend more time building relationships with their students. Teachers put in more work than most people realize, but the vast majority of them feel that it is worth it to have the chance to make a difference in the life of a child.

CAREERS WORKING IN SCHOOLS

Within schools, there are a wide range of careers and salaries. While TSS workers work in schools, they are typically employed by outside agencies that contract with the special-needs student's family. TSS workers usually make $11–$12 per hour, and the number of hours they are permitted to work per week is determined by the organization by which they are employed.

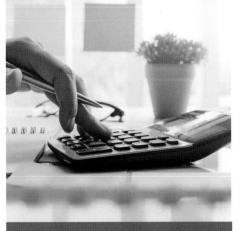

Instructional aides typically make around $23,000 per year, with a potential to earn a much higher salary if they are **bilingual**.

Teachers typically make around $46,000 per year, plus extra if they coach an athletic team or run an after-school club. Teachers also may be given extra money to pay for their tuition in earning their master's or doctorate degree, depending on school district policy. Many schools find that they are struggling to find qualified math, science, special

Before you choose a career, make sure your choice will enable you to earn a salary that you are comfortable with.

Teachers make a basic salary. However, by running out-of-hours activities, private tutoring, or after-school clubs they can earn extra money.

education, and ESOL teachers, so teachers who are certified to teach in these areas often make more money than teachers who have other specialties.

Speech-language pathologists may work in a variety of settings, but they are most typically found employed by schools. They make an average of $75,000 per year.

CAREERS WORKING IN SOCIAL SERVICES

Social workers can be employed in a variety of different environments, including state government, local government, schools, hospitals, and charitable organizations. Social workers typically make about $45,000 per

Careers in social services vary greatly, and consequently, the salaries can be variable too.

year. Child protective services workers fit into this category as well, as most of them are social workers with additional training. Family support workers typically make around $33,000 per year.

CAREERS WORKING IN HOSPITALS

While pediatricians and psychiatrists have to go through an extensive amount of schooling before they are able to work, they are some of the highest earners in the field of working with children. On average, pediatricians make $146,000 per year, and psychiatrists make $198,000 per year.

These numbers sound exciting, but it's important to remember that people in these professions have gone through many years of school and typically have large amounts of student loans that they need to pay back. The hours can also be long and unpredictable, especially at the beginning of their careers.

Pediatricians and psychiatrists who work in a hospital environment command good salaries. However, they often work long hours and typically have large student loans to pay back.

CAREERS WORKING IN PRIVATE PRACTICE

Some children's therapists and counselors work in private practice. This means that they have their own office and are able to set their own hours, giving them flexibility in their work-life balance. The salaries in private practice vary greatly, since different professionals choose to work a different number of hours per week. In general, the salary of a children's therapist or counselor averages around $40,000 in private practice. This number can be much higher for therapists who get their start working in a school or hospital and then transition to private practice, since it's likely that they will already have a base of clients who are willing to pay for their services.

JOB OUTLOOK

In recent years, research in education has shown that children achieve more when they get individualized attention, including smaller classes and small instructional groups. This means that the need for teachers is continuing to increase. Many school districts are increasing the number of teachers on staff while making cuts in other areas. Unfortunately, this sometimes means that school counseling and instructional aide positions get cut. While counseling positions are growing in availability in general in the United States and Canada, the number of positions available in schools is not projected to increase in the near future.

The growth trend is positive for pediatricians, psychiatrists, and psychologists. In the United States and Canada, health care is growing quickly. The same growth trend is being seen for mental health professionals, such as counselors and therapists. In recent years, the stigma against mental health has been lessened in the United States and Canada, leading more parents to seek out mental

Therapists or counselors who work in private practice often get better paid than therapists or counselors who work in a hospital environment.

There are many jobs available today that involve helping children. The growth trend for these jobs remains positive.

health services for their children. This has led to an uptick in available positions for mental health professionals.

WORK SATISFACTION

Like many service professions, burnout is a concern among those who work with children. Burnout is a condition when a person becomes too overwhelmed with the stresses of their job to continue to do the job well. Burnout is especially common in jobs where professionals do not feel that they are fairly compensated for the amount of work that they do, such as teaching and social work.

That being said, many teachers and social workers report extremely high levels of job satisfaction. Early childhood and elementary school teachers are found to be especially happy with their jobs due to the **autonomy** that they

While working in professions that help children can be demanding and sometimes stressful, teaching is one career choice where job satisfaction levels are extremely high.

have over their classrooms. Counselors, therapists, and speech-language pathologists report medium to high levels of job satisfaction as well. Pediatricians report extremely high job satisfaction, and it's theorized that is due to the high amount of time they spend in direct patient care.

One of the main complaints of teachers and social workers is that they spend a lot of time doing paperwork. Most of them feel that their time could better be spent helping children directly. People in these professions can feel frustrated when children need their help and they are stuck in the office filling out forms.

If you choose to work with children, it's important that you utilize self-care to protect yourself against burnout. It's important to only work from home when necessary, and not to get in the habit of working until you go to bed. If you feel that you're especially stressed for a long period of time, talk with your supervisor about creating a plan to lighten your workload so you're still able to perform your job effectively. It's also important to note that there is nothing wrong with using sick days and vacation days—they exist for a reason! Working with children can be stressful, and like with any job, it's important to take care of yourself so that you're able to take care of others.

Successful professionals who work with children do not need to be parents themselves.

DO YOU HAVE TO BE A PARENT TO DO A GOOD JOB WORKING WITH KIDS?

In a word: No! Many successful teachers, counselors, and therapists do not have children. Some never want to have children, and some eventually want to start a family. There is a misconception that it's not easy to work with children unless you have or want to have your own, but nothing could be further from the truth. Professionals with experience working with children and the right education can be successful in the classroom, hospital, or counseling office without having their own children at home.

PLAY THERAPY

See what it's like to be a play therapist

1. On average, how much do social workers make each year?

2. Which of the jobs discussed in this chapter requires the most schooling?

3. What is burnout?

RESEARCH PROJECT

Choose two of the jobs discussed in this chapter, and do additional research to compare and contrast the two. What education is required? How do the work hours differ? How does job satisfaction differ? After doing your research, explain which job you think would be a better fit for you.

SERIES GLOSSARY OF KEY TERMS

abuse: Wrong or unfair treatment or use.

academic: Of or relating to schools and education.

advancement: Progression to a higher stage of development.

anxiety: Fear or nervousness about what might happen.

apprentice: A person who learns a job or skill by working for a fixed period of time for someone who is very good at that job or skill.

culture: A way of thinking, behaving, or working that exists in a place or organization (such as a business).

donation: The making of an especially charitable gift.

empathy: The ability to understand and share the feelings of others.

endangered species: A specific type of plant or animal that is likely to become extinct In the near future.

ethics: The study of morality, or right and wrong.

food security: Having reliable access to a steady source of nutritious food.

intern: A student or recent graduate in a special field of study (such as medicine or teaching) who works for a period of time to gain practical experience.

mediation: Intervention between conflicting parties to promote reconciliation, settlement, or compromise.

nonprofit: A charitable organization that uses its money to help others, rather than to make financial gain, aka "profit."

ombudsman: A person who advocates for the needs and wants of an individual in a facility anonymously so that the individual receiving care can voice complaints without fear of consequences.

pediatrician: A doctor who specializes in the care of babies and children.

perpetrator: A person who commits a harmful or illegal act.

poverty: The state of one who lacks a usual or socially acceptable amount of money or material possessions.

retaliate: To do something bad to someone who has hurt you or treated you badly; to get revenge against someone.

salary: The amount of money you receive each year for the work you perform.

sanctuary: A place of refuge and protection.

stress: Something that causes strong feelings of worry or anxiety.

substance abuse: Excessive use of a drug (such as alcohol, narcotics, or cocaine); use of a drug without medical justification.

syndrome: A group of signs and symptoms that occur together and characterize a particular abnormality or condition.

therapist: A person trained in methods of treatment and rehabilitation other than the use of drugs or surgery.

ORGANIZATIONS TO CONTACT

American Psychological Association: 750 1st St. NE, Washington, DC 20002 Phone: (202) 336-5500 E-mail: info@apa.org
Website: www.apa.org

American School Counselor Association: 1101 King St., Suite 310, Alexandria, VA 22314 Phone: (703) 683-ASCA
E-mail: asca@schoolcounselor.org
Website: www.schoolcounselor.org

Association for Play Therapy: 401 Clovis Ave., Suite 107, Clovis, CA 93612 Phone: (559) 298-3400 E-mail: info@a4pt.org
Website: www.a4pt.org

City Year: 287 Columbus Ave., Boston, MA 02116 Phone: (617) 927-2500 E-mail: corporate@cityyear.org
Website: www.cityyear.org

Shatterproof: 135 West 41st St., 6th Floor, New York, NY 10036
Phone: 1 (800) 597-2557
Website: www.shatterproof.org

The New Teacher Project: 500 7th Ave., 8th Floor, New York, NY 10018
Phone: (718) 233-2800 E-mail: info@tntp.org
Website: www.tntp.org

INTERNET RESOURCES

https://www.apa.org/pi/families/index.aspx
The American Psychological Association's Children, Youth, and Families website provides a plethora or resources regarding the advancement of the science of child development.

https://childmind.org/
The Child Mind Institute is an independent, nonprofit organization that strives to transform the lives of children and families living with behavioral and learning disorders.

https://effectivechildtherapy.org
The Society of Clinical Child and Adolescent Psychology provides therapists, pediatricians, teachers, and other professionals who work with children with evidence-based information on children's psychology.

https://infoaboutkids.org
InfoAboutKids is an ongoing collaboration between a number of organizations that study child and family development. Their site includes research and resources for professionals who work with children.

https://californiateach.org
Are you interested in becoming a teacher? Learn more about what it takes to become an early childhood, elementary, middle, or high school teacher.

FURTHER READING

Ashworth, Mary. *The First Step on the Longer Path: Becoming an ESL Teacher.* Ontario: Pippin Publishing, 2000.

McGuire, Victor. *Conversations about Being a Teacher.* Denver, CO.: Velocity Leadership Consulting, 2017.

Miller, W. Hans. *Soothing: Lives of a Child Psychologist.* Bloomington, IN: XLIBRIS, 2017.

Powell, William and Ochan Kusama-Powell. *Becoming an Emotionally Intelligent Teacher.* New York City: Skyhorse Publishing, 2013.

West, Susan. *How to Become a Social Worker: The Ultimate Guide to Becoming a Social Worker.* Kings Hill: How2Become Ltd. UK, 2015.

INDEX

AUTHOR'S BIOGRAPHY

AMANDA TURNER lives in Dayton, Ohio, with her husband, son, dog, and cat. A former middle school teacher, she now enjoys traveling the country with her family wherever the Air Force chooses to send them! Amanda earned her BA in Psychology from Penn State University and her MEd. in school and mental health counseling from the University of Pennsylvania. During graduate school, Amanda completed an internship counseling patients through drug and alcohol detox.

CREDITS